This book

BELONGS TO

....

Published in 2022 by Welbeck Editions
An imprint of Welbeck Children's Limited,
part of Welbeck Publishing Group
Based in London and Sydney.
www.welbeckpublishing.com

Associate Publisher: Laura Knowles
Commissioning Editor: Bryony Davies
Art Editor: Deborah Vickers
Designer: Ceri Woods
Production: Melanie Robertson
Consultant: Chris Thorogood

ISBN: 978-1-80338-012-4

Printed in Heshan, China

10 9 8 7 6 5 4 3 2 1

FSC
www.fsc.org
MIX
Paper from
responsible sources
FSC® C020056

AROUND the WORLD in 80 TREES

Written by
BEN LERWILL

Illustrated by
KAJA KAJFEŽ

WELBECK
EDITIONS

CONTENTS

A world of trees

Trees are a vital part of life on Earth. They have been on our planet for over 380 million years—dinosaurs would have chewed leaves from their branches! Today they still grow almost everywhere, from chattering rain forests and icy woodlands to tropical islands.

Trees are wonders of nature: they stretch their branches high into the sky and their roots deep into the soil. They come in every shape and size, but they all have roots, a trunk, and leaves, and they need light, water, and a gas called carbon dioxide to survive. They make their own food—a sugary goo called sap. And they release oxygen, which all humans and animals need to breathe.

Trees have been prized by humans since the Stone Age and are still important in cultures around the world. They give us food, materials, shelter, and medicine. They stand proud in our towns, cities, villages, and gardens. In some cultures, they're even seen as holy.

Trees help keep our air cool and moist, and they make our world a better, cleaner place to live in. It's very important that we look after our trees and forests—for our wildlife, for the environment, and for ourselves. They need our care.

Trees are the oldest living things in the world. Some trees alive today are thousands of years old, which means they've been standing in exactly the same spot since the days of the Roman Empire!

7

Types of trees

Trees grow all around the world, ranging in size from miniature willows to mighty redwoods. In total, our planet has more than 60,000 different tree species, and experts think there are more than THREE TRILLION individual trees growing right now.

Parts of a tree

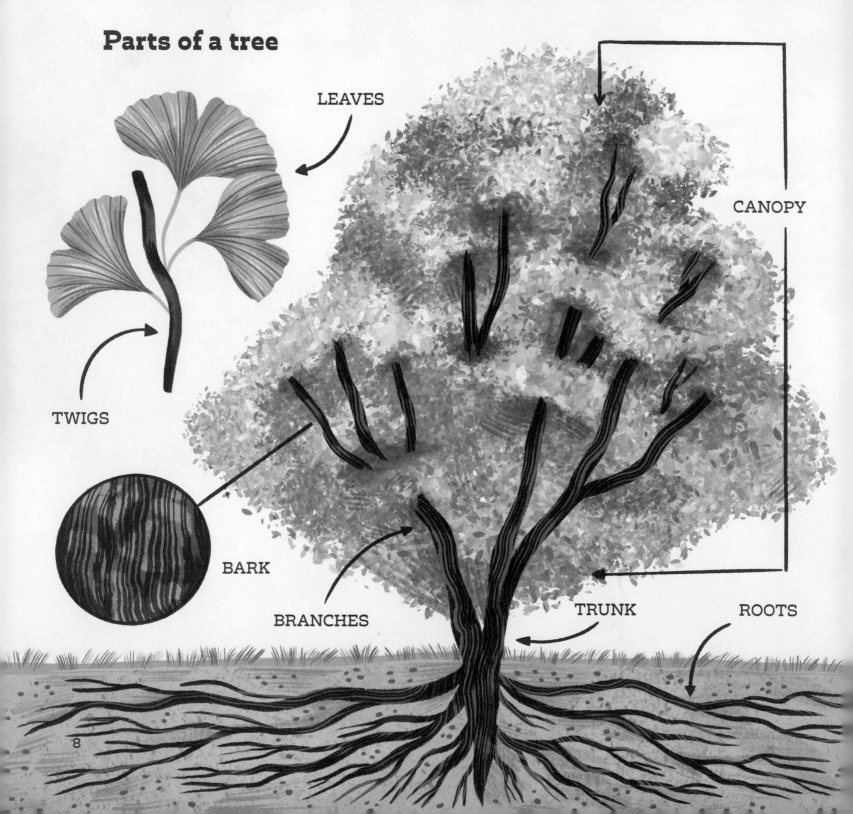

LEAVES

TWIGS

BARK

BRANCHES

CANOPY

TRUNK

ROOTS

8

Coniferous or broadleaf?

Of the huge numbers of trees around the world, most belong to two types of trees: coniferous and broadleaf.

Coniferous trees often have leaves that are thin, spiky needles. They grow in large numbers in colder regions, but we can find them in warm places too. Most coniferous trees are evergreen, which means they keep their needles on their branches all year round. These trees produce their seeds inside cones.

SPRING   SUMMER   AUTUMN   WINTER

Many **broadleaf** trees in colder parts of the world are deciduous, which means they drop their leaves every year and grow new ones again the following spring. As their name suggests, they have leaves that are often wider and flatter than needles—sometimes much wider. These trees usually produce fruits, including nuts, which have seeds inside.

SPRING   SUMMER   AUTUMN   WINTER

The AMERICAS

North and South America are home to some of the most dramatic sights on the planet. The wolf-prowled wilderness of the frozen north and the sweltering green of the Amazon rain forest; the bright lights of New York City and the sandy beaches of Rio de Janeiro; the towering cliffs of the Grand Canyon and the remote hills of Patagonia. These two continents pack in spectacular landscapes, modern cities—and a colossal number of trees. You'll find the world's oldest, widest, and tallest trees here, as well as jumbo conifers, mountain hardwoods, and tropical trees.

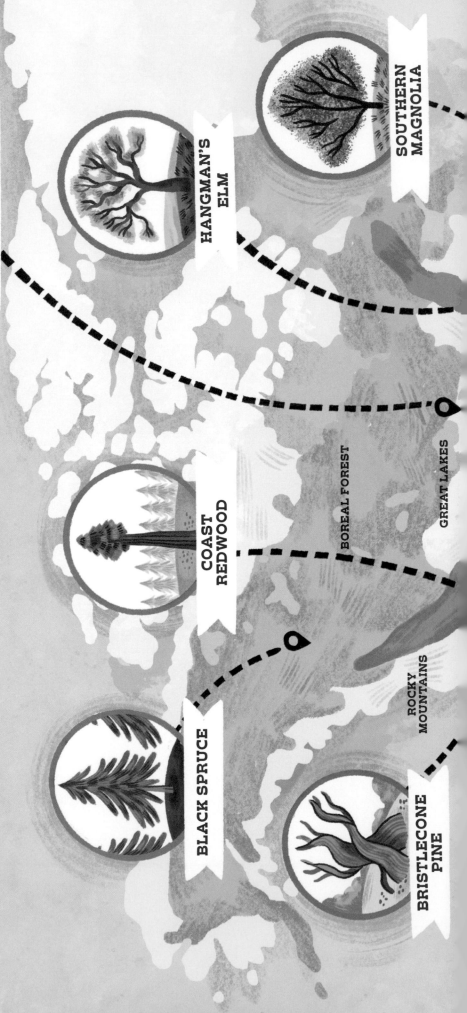

SUGAR MAPLE

HANGMAN'S ELM

SOUTHERN MAGNOLIA

COAST REDWOOD

BOREAL FOREST

GREAT LAKES

BLACK SPRUCE

ROCKY MOUNTAINS

BRISTLECONE PINE

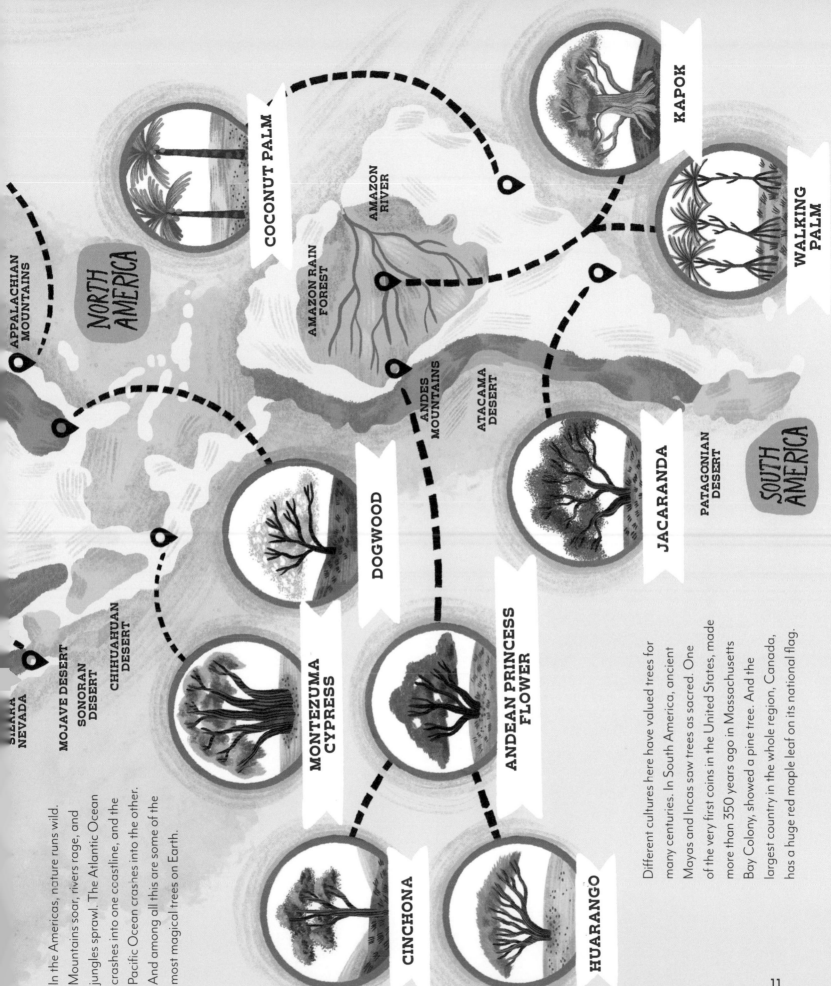

In the Americas, nature runs wild. Mountains soar, rivers rage, and jungles sprawl. The Atlantic Ocean crashes into one coastline, and the Pacific Ocean crashes into the other. And among all this are some of the most magical trees on Earth.

Different cultures here have valued trees for many centuries. In South America, ancient Mayas and Incas saw trees as sacred. One of the very first coins in the United States, made more than 350 years ago in Massachusetts Bay Colony, showed a pine tree. And the largest country in the whole region, Canada, has a huge red maple leaf on its national flag.

NORTH AMERICA

SOUTH AMERICA

APPALACHIAN MOUNTAINS

SIERRA NEVADA

MOJAVE DESERT

SONORAN DESERT

CHIHUAHUAN DESERT

AMAZON RIVER

AMAZON RAIN FOREST

ANDES MOUNTAINS

ATACAMA DESERT

PATAGONIAN DESERT

COCONUT PALM

KAPOK

WALKING PALM

DOGWOOD

JACARANDA

MONTEZUMA CYPRESS

ANDEAN PRINCESS FLOWER

CINCHONA

HUARANGO

11

1. Black spruce

Birdsong echoes through the woods. A cold breeze whistles in the branches. Animals snuffle through the undergrowth. In the middle of it all stands a group of black spruce trees, which grow widely in the chilly forests of northern Canada. Each tree has a dark, scaly trunk and a tight jumble of blue-green needles.

Black spruce trees use their waxy needles to store water, which helps them survive year-round. The winters here are long, dark, and freezing.

The black spruce has small, neat cones that can stay on the branch for as long as 30 years. The cones drop seeds that are happily gobbled up by red squirrels and birds like nuthatches and crossbills.

First Nations people have lived in Canada for thousands of years. They traditionally used the resin from black spruce trees as a kind of chewing gum.

Canada's boreal (or northern) forest stretches almost all the way across this enormous country. It's full of spruce, fir, pine, and aspen, as well as lakes and wetlands—and the occasional family of bears!

Caribou use black spruce trees as shelter when it's snowing, Canada grouse like eating the tree's needles, and mice and hares love nibbling on its young shoots. So while this tree might be skinny—and even a little scruffy—it's a special one.

City trees

The cities and towns of North and South America come in all shapes and sizes—just like their trees.

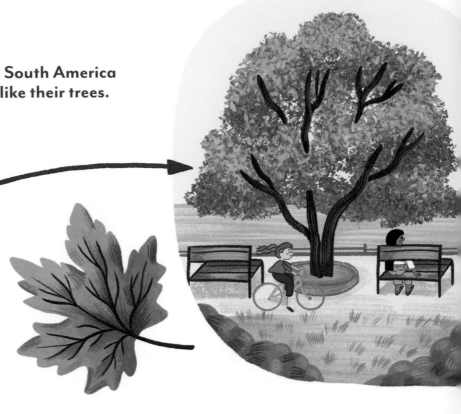

2. Sugar maple

Trees are everywhere in the colorful Canadian city of Toronto. Some have been introduced from other parts of the world, but others are native, like this handsome sugar maple. The tree grows well in parks, and its sap can be used to make maple syrup—perfect for drizzling on pancakes.

3. Dogwood

This pretty, fast-growing tree has become so common in Atlanta, Georgia, that locals hold a two-day dogwood festival every year. Its flowers are large, pale, and showy, but its fruit isn't quite as appealing—some people say the tree was named because its berries taste so terrible that not even dogs eat them!

4. Hangman's elm

Above the hustle and bustle of New York City's Washington Square stands this sturdy elm. Elms are one of America's most popular urban trees, but they're sadly at risk from disease. This New York tree has been here for more than 300 years—longer than the park!—and there are whispers it was once used to hang criminals.

5. Southern magnolia →

With its dark, glossy leaves and wide branches, a magnolia makes for a magnificent sight. This one was planted outside the White House—the home of the President of the United States—back in 1829. A lot of work has been done to keep it healthy, and it's still here today, standing as a leafy part of American history.

6. Montezuma cypress

In the Mexican town of Santa María del Tule stands a tree so thick that it takes about 40 children, all holding hands, to form a ring around it. That's one huge hug! This mammoth Montezuma cypress is thought to be over 1,000 years old, and one legend says it was planted as an offering to an Aztec wind god.

7. Jacaranda →

The capital of Argentina is buzzing Buenos Aires, where the streets crawl with traffic and the cafés chatter with life. But it's not just a human city. Along many of its avenues and squares you'll find rows of jacaranda—a native South American tree that bursts to life each November with purple flowers as light and bright as confetti.

8. Coconut palm

Here in sunny Rio de Janeiro, Brazil, coconut palms have been planted to gaze out over the long, powdery beaches. Originally from the southwest Pacific, they can grow in sand and enjoy the breezy, salty conditions. The tree gives us coconuts, and its leaves can be used to thatch roofs.

Record breakers

Ladies and gentlemen, welcome to the state of California—home of the oldest and tallest trees on planet Earth!

9. Bristlecone pine

This bristlecone pine might be gnarled and twisty, but it's been growing here in California's White Mountains for more than 4,850 years. The tree has been given the name Methuselah (after a man in the Bible who lived to the grand old age of 969), and it is officially the world's oldest named individual tree. When the pyramids were being built in Egypt, this plucky pine was approaching its 300th birthday!

One of the things that makes this tree so remarkable is where it's found. Growing at about 10,000 feet above sea level, it spends some of the year under snow and the rest of the year frazzled by hot sunshine. Incredibly, this stress seems to make the tree stronger. It also has some very old neighbors, with other ancient bristlecone pines growing close by. However, these famous trees are very difficult to find—because Methuselah's exact location is a secret!

10. Coast redwood

Crane your neck up, and up, and up. The thick, towering trunk you see here belongs to a coast redwood nicknamed Hyperion. The tip of its crown stretches about 380 feet above the forest floor, making it the tallest known tree in the world. Not even Big Ben's tower or the Statue of Liberty come close to matching it for height, and scientists think this extralarge evergreen could be up to 800 years old.

Redwoods are the largest trees on the planet. They grow so big in California because they get the perfect mix of sun and rain, and the rich soil is just right for them. They also wear a special armor: coast redwoods like Hyperion have trunks that are a warm red-brown color, and their chunky bark is tough enough to resist insects, fungi, and even fire. This makes the coast redwood a true titan of the natural world.

17

The Amazon rain forest

Almost 400 billion trees grow here in the tropical heat of the world's biggest rain forest—including these seven species.

11. Rubber tree

There's more to this bushy tree than you might think. When its bark is cut, a white, milky sap called latex oozes out. After it's treated, this latex turns into a natural rubber that can be used for tires, shoes, and many other things. The tree also has fruits that reproduce by exploding when they're ripe in order to scatter their seeds far across the forest floor.

12. Walking palm

Balancing on skinny roots, this unusual plant looks like a tree with lots of little legs. It has even been suggested that by growing new roots, the tree can "walk" through the jungle, inch by inch, to find more sunlight and better soil. Some experts think this is nonsense. What's certain is that if walking palms do move, they make even sloths look speedy!

13. Barrigona

The word "barrigona" translates as "pot-bellied," so it's is a fitting name for this tall, common rain forest tree that has a tummy-bulge halfway up its trunk. Astonishingly, there are more than four billion of them in the Amazon! This is good news for tapirs, toucans, and spider monkeys, who all like eating the tree's soft-centered fruits.

14. Kapok

A real giant of the jungle, the kapok grows so large that when it reaches full size, the tree is as wide as it is tall. Its heavy branches shoot off from the trunk at right angles, and the crevices around its roots are perfect hiding places for birds and frogs. In parts of the Amazon, this mighty tree is regarded as the father of all animals.

15. Cacao

Now here's a rain forest tree to be grateful for . . . especially if you have a sweet tooth. The cacao tree has a thick crown of leathery leaves, but what really makes it special are the colorful pods that grow on its branches. These pods each contain between 50 and 100 cocoa beans—the main ingredient in chocolate!

Hungry agoutis feast on Brazil nuts.

16. Brazil nut

Teetering high above the ground on a bare, narrow trunk, the Brazil nut tree grows wild across the Amazon. Its name comes from the chunky nuts that it produces. They're tasty to humans and a treat for furry mammals called agoutis, who use their sharp teeth to gobble them up. Like squirrels with acorns, they even bury some!

17. Balsa

We usually think of wood as being heavy, but the pale wood from the balsa tree is the lightest in the world—so light that it's used for floats, rafts, and even model airplanes. The tree itself grows incredibly fast, shooting up 10 feet in just six months, and like many tropical plants, its flowers are pollinated by bats.

The Andes

The Andes Mountains stretch all the way down South America, playing host to snow-capped peaks, spectacular wildlife —and some remarkable trees.

18. Polylepis

Up in the highest parts of the Andes, where condors soar through the thin air, only a few tree species can survive. At the top of the list is the polylepis, a sturdy evergreen that can live for more than 700 years and grows higher up than any other broadleaf tree in the world. Very few insects live up here, so the tree is pollinated by the wind.

19. Monkey puzzle

You wouldn't want to climb this spiky mountain tree—it got its name because even monkeys would struggle to clamber through its stiff, prickly branches! But it's like this for a reason. Monkey puzzles have been growing here in the Andes for 200 million years, and their sharp leaves meant that hungry dinosaurs left them alone and grazed on other trees.

20. Incadendron

The Inca Trail is a long, ancient path winding through the misty mountains of Peru. People have been walking the trail for more than 500 years, so scientists were amazed when they realized one of the tree species on the path had never been discovered. The incadendron, which was only named in 2017, can reach up to 100 feet in height.

21. Andean princess flower

This eye-catching froth of purple is an Andean princess flower, also known as a glory bush. A small mountain tree with evergreen leaves, it bursts to life for several months each year in a beautiful mass of dazzling, five-petaled flowers.

22. Cinchona

Meet the life-saving cinchona tree. It might look ordinary, but it has a secret: its bark contains a drug called quinine, which for a long time was the only medicine that worked against a disease called malaria. Quinine helped save many soldiers with malaria in World War I, and some doctors still use it today.

23. Huarango

Growing in the bone-dry foothills of the Andes, the huarango tree has an incredible way of surviving. Its roots can reach down into the soil for more than 160 feet, finding water deep, deep underground. At the same time, its feathery leaves can trap mist, gathering even more moisture. Local people have prized huarango trees for thousands of years.

24. Antarctic beech

This South American tree isn't found in Antarctica itself (the great icy continent has no trees at all, which makes life tough for its poor, windswept penguins), but it gets its name because it grows farther south than almost any other tree species on Earth. As well as being found on mountains, it also grows at sea level, and its leaves turn a beautiful bronze in the autumn.

Leaves

All trees need leaves. Some are short and flat, others are big and floppy. Some have curvy edges, others have spiky sides. But what they all have in common is that they perform a vital job for their trees. And remember, needles are leaves too!

Why are leaves so important?

They absorb air and light, which trees need to survive.

Leaves "breathe in" carbon dioxide from the air and "breathe out" the special gas that we all need to survive: oxygen!

All leaves contain a natural green color called chlorophyll. They use this chlorophyll to soak up energy from sunlight. Together with water from the soil, this helps them make a sugary food for the tree.

Leaves have veins, which act as little pipelines to carry food and water to and from other parts of the tree. Even needles have tiny veins.

Big and small

Different leaves have different powers. Rain forest leaves are often very wide and round, to help them draw in as much air and sunlight as possible. The tree with the biggest leaves in the world is the raffia palm. Its leaves can grow up to 80 feet long—that's longer than a tennis court! Pine needles, however, are strong and thin, which lets them hold water and also means they don't get blown around too much in a storm.

Why do some trees drop their leaves?

Many broadleaf trees in colder parts of the globe are deciduous, which means their leaves fall off each year when summer has finished. These trees don't need their leaves over the winter, when there's less sunlight for them to absorb. There's also a danger that the water in the leaves might freeze in the cold. So as autumn begins, the trees start to "let go" of the leaves.

When this happens, the chlorophyll's green color begins to fade and the leaves begin to turn red, or orange, or yellow, before eventually falling to the ground. When spring arrives a few months later, the trees grow a whole crown of brand-new green leaves—in time for another busy season of soaking up carbon dioxide and sunlight.

Most conifers, like firs and pines, are evergreen and keep their leaves all year round. This is because their leaves are needles, and their waxy coat means the water inside them doesn't freeze.

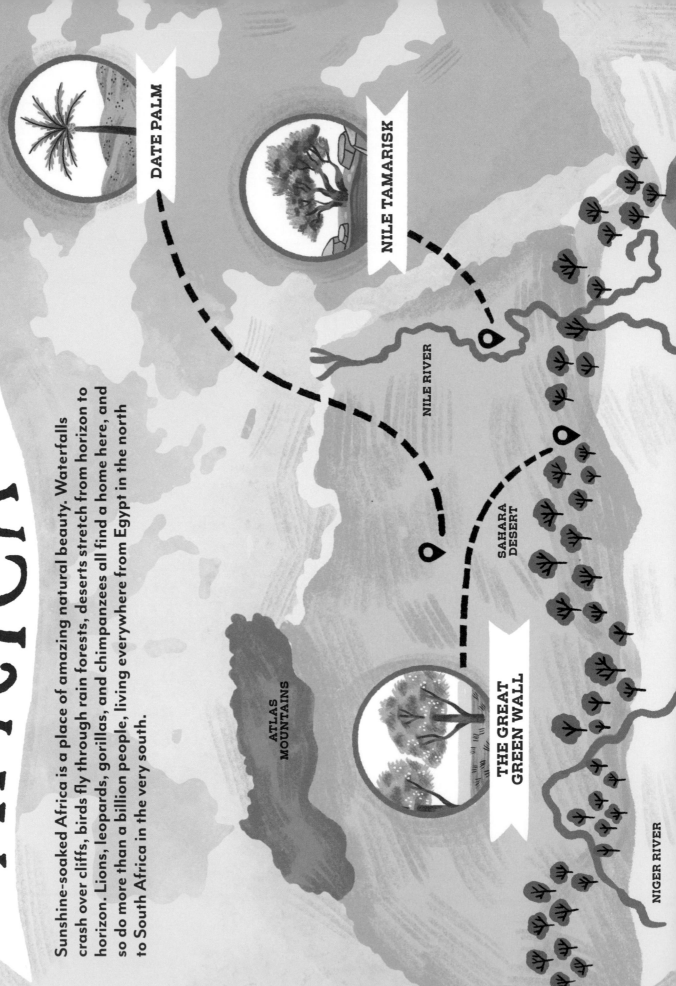

AFRICA

Sunshine-soaked Africa is a place of amazing natural beauty. Waterfalls crash over cliffs, birds fly through rain forests, deserts stretch from horizon to horizon. Lions, leopards, gorillas, and chimpanzees all find a home here, and so do more than a billion people, living everywhere from Egypt in the north to South Africa in the very south.

DATE PALM

NILE TAMARISK

NILE RIVER

SAHARA DESERT

ATLAS MOUNTAINS

THE GREAT GREEN WALL

NIGER RIVER

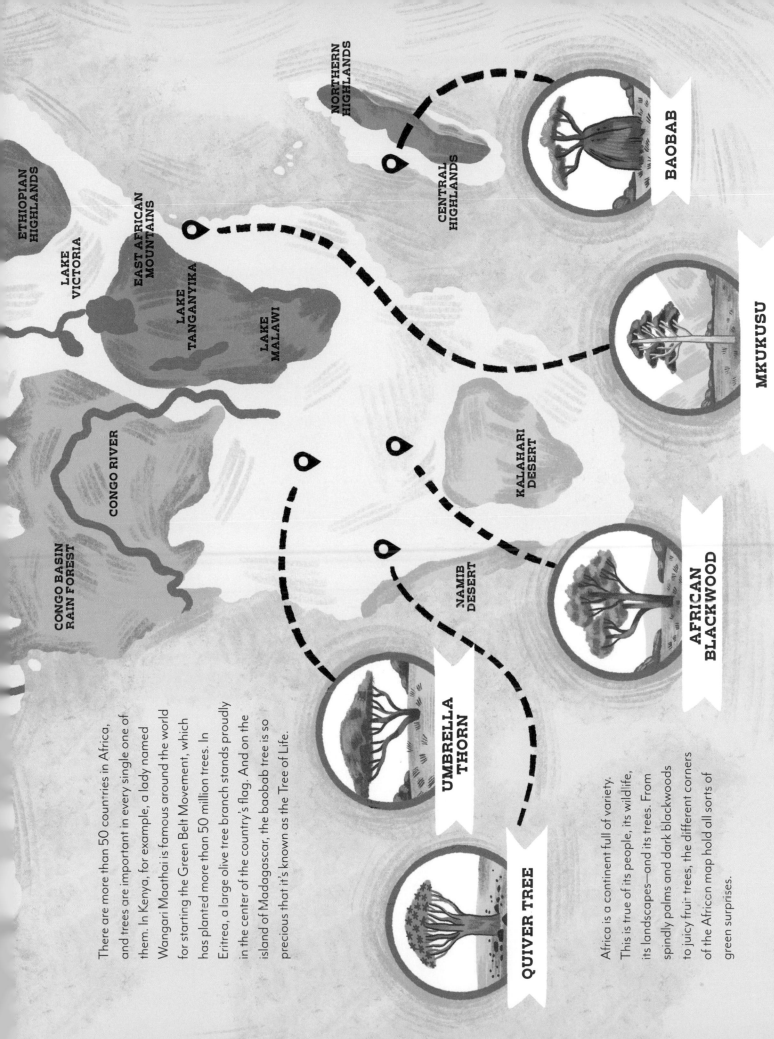

ETHIOPIAN HIGHLANDS

LAKE VICTORIA

EAST AFRICAN MOUNTAINS

CONGO RIVER

CONGO BASIN RAIN FOREST

LAKE TANGANYIKA

LAKE MALAWI

NORTHERN HIGHLANDS

CENTRAL HIGHLANDS

KALAHARI DESERT

NAMIB DESERT

BAOBAB

MKUKUSU

AFRICAN BLACKWOOD

UMBRELLA THORN

QUIVER TREE

There are more than 50 countries in Africa, and trees are important in every single one of them. In Kenya, for example, a lady named Wangari Maathai is famous around the world for starting the Green Belt Movement, which has planted more than 50 million trees. In Eritrea, a large olive tree branch stands proudly in the center of the country's flag. And on the island of Madagascar, the baobab tree is so precious that it's known as the Tree of Life.

Africa is a continent full of variety. This is true of its people, its wildlife, its landscapes—and its trees. From spindly palms and dark blackwoods to juicy fruit trees, the different corners of the African map hold all sorts of green surprises.

25

North Africa

North Africa is huge, hot, and dominated by the dunes of the Sahara desert, but many tree species still manage to grow here.

25. Desert date

Have you ever heard of the Great Green Wall? It's a wonderful plan to plant a row of trees all the way across North Africa—for 5,000 miles! The project is helping the environment and bringing jobs to local people. Tens of thousands of trees have already been planted, including many desert dates. These thorny trees can go for two whole years without water.

26. Argan

Many animals climb trees to find food . . . but they're not often goats! Here in Morocco, the fleshy fruits of the argan tree are irresistible to these brave goats, who balance on branches to find a meal. And that's not all—the fruits also contain a very valuable oil that can help humans who have dry or flaky skin.

27. Nile tamarisk

The Nile is one of the longest rivers in the world, flowing from the heart of Africa all the way up to the Mediterranean Sea. In Egypt, where the river passes mighty pyramids and tombs, Nile tamarisk trees grow on its banks. These trees might be small, but they've seen thousands of years of Egyptian history drifting under their branches.

28. Bitter orange

The Moroccan city of Marrakech is full of tight, crowded lanes where spices fill the air, but search closely and you'll find something greener. Hidden in its peaceful courtyards are glossy orange trees, originally from Asia, with fruits that glow like jewels. Don't eat them straight from the tree, though—these bitter oranges taste best when they're in marmalade!

29. Shea

This bushy tree has long green leaves and is often found in the country of Mali. It's famous for the "butter" that can be ground from its nuts. Shea butter is full of healthy fat, making it good for cooking and for rubbing onto your skin to keep it moist. The tree is also vital for a special type of caterpillar that only eats shea leaves.

30. Saharan cypress

This rare conifer survives with a few others on a rocky mountain, where just a few drops of rain a year are enough to keep it alive. Just as impressively, this tall, thirsty evergreen can grow here in the desert for more than 1,000 years.

31. Date palm

Huge numbers of these stocky palm trees have been planted across North Africa, where their sweet, sticky fruits are very popular. You can sometimes find more than 1,000 dates in a single bunch! These palms have been planted for food for a whopping 5,000 years, so when you eat a date, you're enjoying the same snack as people who lived long, long ago.

Baobabs grow in many parts of the African continent, although six of the seven baobab species are found only on the island of Madagascar. In a world packed with wonderful trees, the baobab—which can live for more than 3,000 years and grow to the size of a seven-story building—is a truly special sight.

These mammoth trees are treasured. In Madagascar, their size and strength means that many local people see them as sacred, or holy. Some even leave gifts of honey, candy, or money at the base of baobab trunks.

32. Baobab

The baobab is no ordinary tree. Big, bulging, and bizarre, it looks like a giant elephant's leg rising from the soil, a tropical tower of bark and branches. The thickness of its trunk lets it store lots of water, which is vital in hot places that sometimes go months without rain. Because its curly branches look like roots, the baobab is sometimes called the upside-down tree!

Unusually, the baobab's large white flowers open up at night, when they get pollinated by bats and nocturnal insects like moths.

Baobabs are important for wildlife too. In some parts of Africa, monkeys and warthogs like eating the seeds and fruits, and thirsty elephants sometimes chew the soft, moist bark.

The baobab's bark is so strong that some people peel it off to make ropes, nets, bags—and even houses. The good news is that the bark always grows back!

Southern Africa

The southern half of the continent is a place of big cities, wide landscapes, and colorful wildlife—and some truly tremendous trees.

33. Quiver tree

With its lumpy trunk, snaking branches, and spiky leaves, the quiver tree is a very curious sight. It's found in some of the driest parts of Namibia and South Africa, growing arrow-straight into the hot blue skies. And funnily enough, it gets its name because people used to hollow out its branches and use them as quivers, which are carriers for arrows!

34. Iroko

Stretching high above the ground on a strong, slender trunk, the iroko is one of the most prized trees in Africa. With wood so hard that not even termites can burrow through it, the tree is just the right thing for furniture makers. It also grows soft wild fruits—a filling snack for bats and squirrels.

35. Mkukusu

Dozens of these towering trees look out across the wilderness from the shadow of Mount Kilimanjaro, Africa's mightiest peak—and the mkukusu has a big, big trunk to match the big, big mountain. It can reach heights of more than 260 feet—that's as tall as 15 adult giraffes!

36. Sausage tree

No prizes for guessing how this tropical tree gets its name! Its droopy, sausage-shaped fruits are actually poisonous, although the tree's blood-red flowers are delicious to impalas, baboons, and other animals. Interestingly, the tree can be either deciduous or evergreen—in dry places it loses its leaves each year, but in rainy areas it keeps them!

37. Mopane

The mopane is best known for its bright green, butterfly-shaped leaves—but it also has an amazing trick. If its branches are being browsed by a hungry elephant, the tree sends a bitter substance to the leaves to make them taste bad. Even more cleverly, it releases a chemical onto the wind to let nearby mopane trees know that elephants are around!

38. Marula

These broadleaf trees have been growing here in Africa for at least 10,000 years, and their plum-sized fruits have always been an important food for humans and animals. In Zimbabwe, in a cave once used by local tribes, scientists found the stones of an amazing 24 million marula fruits! They hold more vitamin C than mangoes and oranges.

39. African blackwood

This small, slow-growing tree has one of the darkest and most valuable woods in the world. It sometimes gets used to make musical instruments like clarinets and oboes, but what makes the tree really special is the job it does for the environment. Like certain other trees, with the help of bacteria it can harvest an important gas called nitrogen, which helps keep the soil fertile.

40. Umbrella thorn

It's early evening on the plains of East Africa. Zebras graze in the distance,
a warm breeze ruffles the grass, and birds glimmer across the sky. In the bough
of a tree lies a leopard, its spotted coat glowing in the last of the day's light.
The tree is an umbrella thorn, a kind of acacia tree, and its silhouette is visible
from far in the distance. Its crown is wide and curved, just like an umbrella.

Although these good-looking trees might seem lonely, they play a very important role here on the plains. Vervet monkeys and baboons feed on their seed pods, vultures perch on the highest branches, and weaverbirds dangle their nests from the canopies. In an environment like this, where everything on the plains is connected, the umbrella thorn is a gift from nature.

Giraffes love chewing the umbrella thorn's sweet leaves and even chomp away on the tree's young, soft thorns. When they eat its leaves and seeds, they're also doing an important job. By pooping out the seeds onto other parts of the plains, they're helping new trees grow.

The umbrella thorn tree is related to the whistling thorn tree, which has ants living inside its hollow thorns. When the ants make little exit holes in the thorns, it makes the trees whistle in the wind!

A family tree of trees

Scientists think there are about **400,000** different types of plants in the world—including more than **60,000** tree species. That's a lot of leafy things to make sense of!

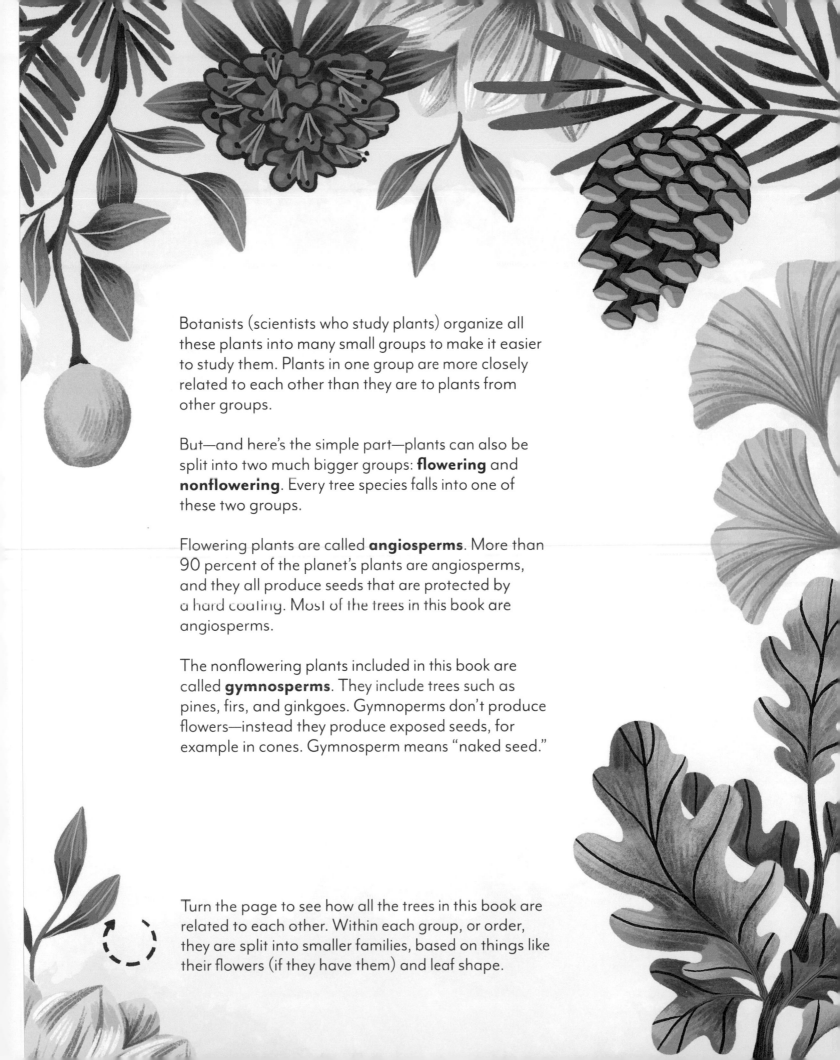

Botanists (scientists who study plants) organize all these plants into many small groups to make it easier to study them. Plants in one group are more closely related to each other than they are to plants from other groups.

But—and here's the simple part—plants can also be split into two much bigger groups: **flowering** and **nonflowering**. Every tree species falls into one of these two groups.

Flowering plants are called **angiosperms**. More than 90 percent of the planet's plants are angiosperms, and they all produce seeds that are protected by a hard coating. Most of the trees in this book are angiosperms.

The nonflowering plants included in this book are called **gymnosperms**. They include trees such as pines, firs, and ginkgoes. Gymnoperms don't produce flowers—instead they produce exposed seeds, for example in cones. Gymnosperm means "naked seed."

Turn the page to see how all the trees in this book are related to each other. Within each group, or order, they are split into smaller families, based on things like their flowers (if they have them) and leaf shape.

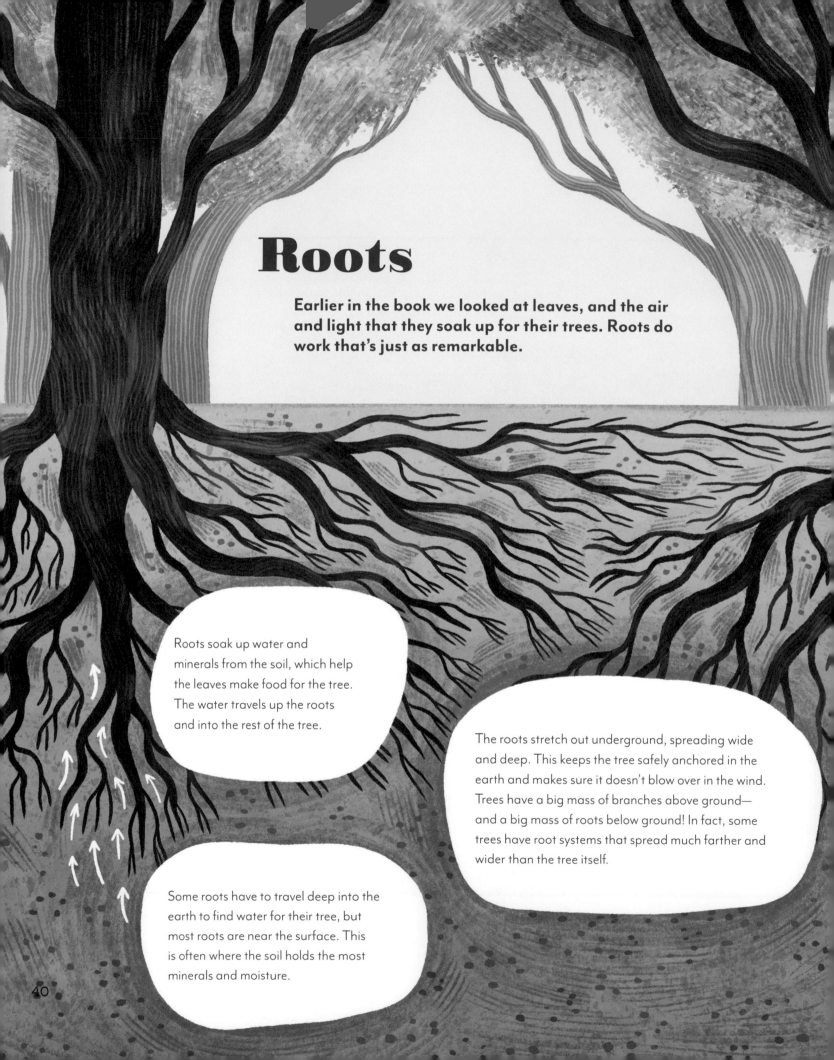

Roots

Earlier in the book we looked at leaves, and the air and light that they soak up for their trees. Roots do work that's just as remarkable.

Roots soak up water and minerals from the soil, which help the leaves make food for the tree. The water travels up the roots and into the rest of the tree.

The roots stretch out underground, spreading wide and deep. This keeps the tree safely anchored in the earth and makes sure it doesn't blow over in the wind. Trees have a big mass of branches above ground— and a big mass of roots below ground! In fact, some trees have root systems that spread much farther and wider than the tree itself.

Some roots have to travel deep into the earth to find water for their tree, but most roots are near the surface. This is often where the soil holds the most minerals and moisture.

Tree teamwork

Maybe the most amazing thing about roots is that they can help trees work as a team. By spreading out, linking together, and using a network of fungi that grows inside and around their roots, trees create a huge underground web, connecting tree to tree.

Trees can use this "web" to share nutrients, to pass sugar and water to weaker trees, and even to warn their neighbors if they're at risk from disease. Some scientists say this is proof that trees can "talk" to each other—and all through their roots!

The taproot is the first root that grows from a tree seed. It is usually the thickest, straightest, and strongest root. Unlike most roots, it grows down (vertically) rather than across (horizontally).

The main roots of a tree are often as big and thick as branches. The smallest can be as thin as strands of hair!

Roots give useful shelter to burrowing animals like rabbits and mice.

NORDMANN FIR

MALUS SIEVERSII

GINKGO

SNOWROSE

LAKE
BAIKAL

GOBI
DESERT

**NEPALESE
RHODODENDRON**

HIMALAYAS

MEKONG
RIVER

FRANKINCENSE

BANYAN

The countries of Europe and Asia are like enormous worlds of their own. Think of China, with its ancient temples and cloudy forests, or Russia, with its endless plains. And don't forget incredible India, with its holy rivers and sweltering cities. Together they have billions of people, animals—and yes, trees.

There's no ocean between these two continents, but the trees that grow here are amazingly varied—and the food and materials they provide have been central to life since creatures first walked on Earth.

Europe and Asia are crammed with unforgettable landscapes, from the snowy forests of Sweden and the sandy beaches of Spain to the mighty mountains of Nepal and the deep valleys of Oman. Every corner of the map holds life—and where there's life, there are trees.

Europe

Stretching from the freezing Arctic Circle to the warm Mediterranean Sea, Europe is filled with trees of different kinds.

41. Nordmann fir

This shaggy conifer grows wild in the woods—but you might have seen it wrapped in lights and decorations! The Nordmann fir is originally from the remote Caucasus Mountains, on the very edge of Europe, and its shiny green needles and firm branches make it one of the world's most popular Christmas trees. People have been decorating fir trees at Christmas since the 1500s.

42. Olive

Its trunk might be short and its leaves might be leathery, but the olive tree is a vital part of life in hot countries like Spain and Greece. Its smooth, small fruits are green when they first appear, then gradually turn darker on the tree. These olives can be eaten on their own or squeezed to make buttery-gold olive oil.

43. Large-leaved lime

High and graceful with arching branches, the large-leaved lime is one of Europe's loveliest trees. In the town of Velké Opatovice in the Czech Republic, it has a very special role: it was planted back in 1918 to celebrate the end of World War I, and today it's a symbol of freedom.

44. European larch

Red squirrels love eating the seeds of this bushy tree, but they need to be good at climbing. The European larch can grow five times as high as a house! It looks like an evergreen tree, and its needles provide a tasty snack for caterpillars, but every autumn these narrow leaves turn yellow and drop to the forest floor.

45. Copper beech

Who says trees have to be green? Like a splosh of purple paint, this fine-looking tree stands out from the crowd with its waterfall of deep-red leaves. Most beech trees are green, but the copper beech is different—it contains a coloring called anthocyanin that makes the tree look this color! It's often planted in big parks and gardens, where its colorful canopy makes it glow.

46. London plane

Here's a plane that has nothing to do with airports. This tall tree with wide leaves and dappled bark is the most common tree in London, England, because it's strong enough to stay healthy in the big, busy city. Plane trees are also very popular in France, where they stand high above town squares and country roads, giving shade from the summer sun.

47. Common holly

Hooray for holly! This prickly evergreen with ruby-red berries grows in many parts of Europe. The leaves near the ground are sharp and spiky to keep them from being gobbled by grazing animals, but they often become smoother higher up. Birds can nest in its sheltered branches, and bees can find pollen and nectar in its summer flowers.

48. Common oak

This is the faithful giant of the tree world. An oak is handsome and muscular, with ridged bark and a wide crown of branches. Its boughs are thick and huggable, stretching out and away from the main trunk, and its leaves look like they've been cut out neatly with scissors.

An oak can live for more than 1,000 years, so it's seen as a symbol of strength and power in many European countries. The UK, Ireland, and Germany all have an oak as their national tree, and it's also linked to two of the mightiest figures from mythology: the Greek god Zeus and the Norse thunder god, Thor. The tree is so special that some Roman emperors even wore crowns made from oak leaves.

The tree grows best in damp soil and drops fresh acorns every year. Squirrels and jays often bury these nuts away—and if they forget about them, the acorns can sprout into new oak trees!

The famous British ship HMS *Victory* was built in the 1700s using the hard wood from over 2,000 oak trees.

There are over 400 species of oak trees around the world.

Some people roast and boil acorns to make a hot drink known as "acorn coffee." Unsurprisingly, it tastes rather nutty!

When leaves fall from an oak, they slowly turn into a soft bed of leaf mold under the tree. This is a perfect habitat for beetles and mushrooms.

The Middle East

The Middle East, or Western Asia, may have vast deserts, but surprisingly it also has an extraordinary variety of trees.

49. Dragon blood tree

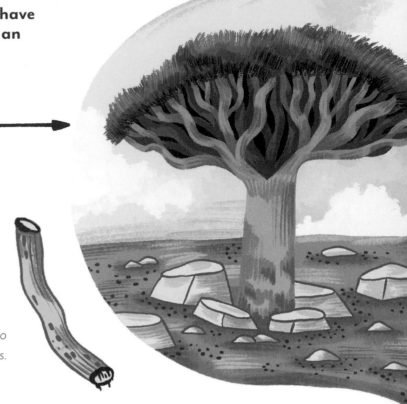

Alien broccoli? A giant mushroom from outer space? This is actually a dragon blood tree, one of the most unusual trees in Asia. The name comes from its dark red sap, which some people use as a kind of medicine for stomach aches. The tree is endemic, which means that it grows only in one place: the magical island of Socotra, in the Arabian Sea.

The tree's blood-red sap can also help with burns, cuts, and rashes.

50. Frankincense

Trees give us all kinds of amazing gifts. These snaking branches and long leaves belong to the frankincense tree, which is famous for its thick, sticky resin (resin is like sap, but gloopier). When it's turned into an oil or perfume, it gives off a deep, wonderful smell. Frankincense resin has been prized for thousands of years.

51. Stinking juniper

Most trees have male and female parts, but every juniper is either a male or a female. And although stinking juniper sounds like a funny insult, this evergreen is definitely a tree to admire. It grows in high, dry, rocky places, and it has dark green clusters of leaves. And the strange name? If its leaves are crushed, they make a nasty odor!

52. Henna

This small tree holds a surprise. Its leaves can be turned into a dark paste called henna dye, which lets people decorate their hands and feet with beautiful red-brown patterns—a lot like temporary tattoos. But making body art with henna is nothing new. It's been used like this for 6,000 years! Historians think Cleopatra even colored her hair with the dye.

53. Common alder

This water-loving tree is found in the cooler parts of the Middle East, often near streams and rivers. The tree's wood becomes stronger and harder when it gets wet. This makes it great for boat building, and in the past it was also used for clogs, or wooden shoes. People once thought that putting alder leaves in their shoes kept their feet from swelling!

54. Cedar of Lebanon

It's hard to think of a more majestic tree than the cedar of Lebanon, with its soaring trunk and wide, elegant branches. The tree has been admired since ancient times, and it still stands proudly in the middle of Lebanon's national flag. Historians think that King Solomon's temple, in Jerusalem, was built from cedar wood more than 2,000 years ago.

55. Jujube

Some religions tell us that the first people on Earth were a man and woman called Adam and Eve, who picked fruit from a tree when they weren't allowed to. Today in Iraq a dead trunk looks out across the Tigris River. Its bare branches were once part of a jujube, a type of fruit tree, and some people believe this is the very same tree from the story.

This bare tree trunk is thought to be the Tree of Knowledge.

56. Cherry

This cloud of snowy pink blossom is a cherry tree in bloom. Japan has these trees in many of its parks and gardens, and every spring their pretty flowers burst to life. People travel from around the country, and sometimes from all over the world, to see them and have parties and picnics under their branches. There's even a special Japanese word—*hanami*—which means "looking at cherry blossoms."

But this spectacular sight doesn't last long. The cherry blossoms only stay on the trees for about a week, before fluttering down to the ground. Several weeks later, the cherries themselves appear—although the tiny fruits aren't big and tasty like the cherries you might find on a cake. Here in Japan, the blossoms are often pickled and eaten by humans or used to flavor cups of tea, but only birds eat the cherries!

Birds help pollinate the cherry trees. Japanese white-eyes like drinking nectar from the flowers with their long, thin beaks.

There are hundreds of different types of cherry trees in Japan, all with slightly different petals and colors. The most common is the Yoshino cherry, with its bright pink blossoms.

Cherry trees have been an important part of Japanese life for hundreds of years. People think the first *hanami* party was held by Toyotomi Hideyoshi, the ruler of the country, way back in 1598!

Japan's rugby team is fast and powerful. The players have cherry flowers on their shirts, and the team's nickname is the Brave Blossoms.

All around Asia

From the wide plains of Central Asia to the cities and forests of the Far East, this is a place with some truly precious trees.

57. Snowrose

Here's a tree that won't even come up to your knee! Snowrose is one of the species used for *bonsai*—a kind of art where people deliberately grow tiny trees that look like bigger ones. The miniature trunks, leaves, and branches need to be treated very carefully. In some countries there are even *bonsai* teachers, who can show you how to take care of the trees.

58. Ginkgo

The fan-shaped leaves of the ginkgo turn a golden yellow each autumn—but the tree's history is even more stunning. Scientists have found ginkgo fossils dating back 200 million years, which means this species was here on Earth before the dinosaurs! Today it's rare to find a ginkgo tree in the wild, but they're still grown in gardens around the world.

59. Nepalese rhododendron

High in the Himalayas, where snowy mountains spear into the sky, you'll find a small tree with dazzling red flowers. This is the Nepalese rhododendron, which explodes into color every spring. Some people even pick and eat the petals, or turn them into a sugary juice. The word rhododendron means "rose tree," and today it's the national flower of Nepal.

60. Weeping willow

Messy or magnificent? The weeping willow is a tree to treasure, with trails of silvery-green leaves that droop down to the ground. Originally found in China, it now grows all around the world. If you've ever explored one, you'll know it also makes a great climbing hideout!

61. *Malus sieversii*

This type of wild apple tree grows in the faraway mountains of Kazakhstan in Central Asia. But what makes it so special? Well, its leaves are thick and its fruits are sweet and juicy, but there's another reason—experts think it was the world's first apple species, which makes it the parent of most of our modern apples. So if you like apples, thank *malus sieversii*!

62. Yellow meranti

Have you ever played Minecraft? If you have, you might have seen this huge tropical tree, which can be grown in the computer game. It's as tall as 65 people standing on top of each other and weighs more than a big airplane. It grows high above the jungles of Malaysia, where you can also find orangutans, forest elephants, and clouded leopards.

63. Soapberry

This Indian tree carries a clue in its name. Its hard round fruits don't taste very nice, but they can keep you clean! The fruit shells contain a natural soap called saponin—people use it to make shampoo, to wash their skin, and even to do their laundry. Bees like the tree too, because its nectar is great for making honey.

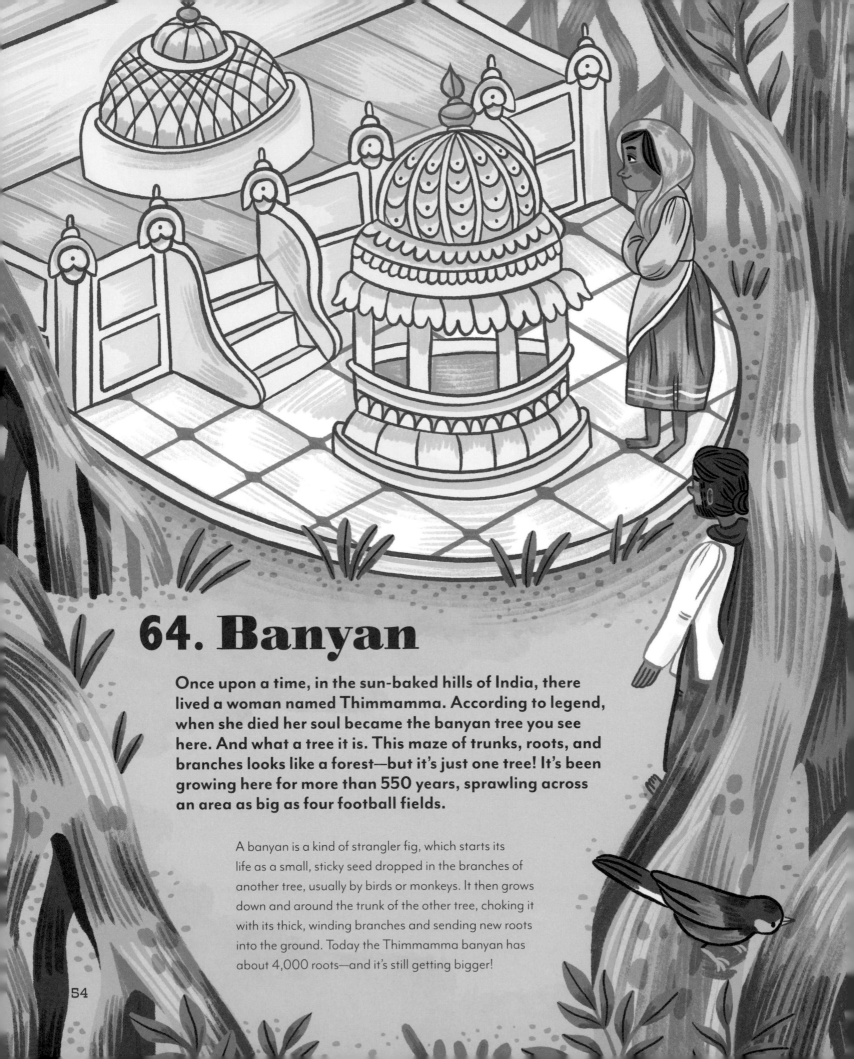

64. Banyan

Once upon a time, in the sun-baked hills of India, there lived a woman named Thimmamma. According to legend, when she died her soul became the banyan tree you see here. And what a tree it is. This maze of trunks, roots, and branches looks like a forest—but it's just one tree! It's been growing here for more than 550 years, sprawling across an area as big as four football fields.

A banyan is a kind of strangler fig, which starts its life as a small, sticky seed dropped in the branches of another tree, usually by birds or monkeys. It then grows down and around the trunk of the other tree, choking it with its thick, winding branches and sending new roots into the ground. Today the Thimmamma banyan has about 4,000 roots—and it's still getting bigger!

The Thimmamma banyan is so important to local people that there's even a small temple deep in its center. It holds statues of Thimmamma and her husband.

All fig trees, including banyans, are pollinated only by tiny fig wasps. The trees can't survive without the wasps, and the wasps can't survive without the trees!

When a banyan "chokes" another tree, it often kills it completely. The better news is that the banyan's sugary figs feed many different animals, like mynah birds and fruit bats.

Pollination, flowers, and seeds

Every tree began its life as a seed. Imagine that! The biggest oak you've ever seen was once a tiny seed inside an acorn. When trees grow flowers, fruits, nuts, and cones, it's their way of making new seeds for new trees to sprout from. But they need the help of small creatures—and sometimes the wind—to make this happen.

What is pollination?

Pollination is how trees make new trees. First, the tree produces flowers, which we often call blossoms. These flowers contain special grains called pollen. When pollen is carried from one flower to another, the second flower has what it needs to become pollinated, which lets it grow into a fruit. Inside the fruit are seeds for new trees.

The **stigma** is sticky. It catches pollen brought from other flowers

The **pollen** is made at the top of the **stamen**

Bright **petals** help attract insects

Nectar is a sugary liquid that insects love

Inside the **ovary** are **ovules**, which develop into seeds after the flower is fertilized

Many trees need insects or other animals to help them spread their pollen. Bees, butterflies, moths, wasps, bats, beetles, and birds are all important pollinators. These insects and animals visit flowers to find a sugary liquid called nectar. While they're drinking the nectar, some of the pollen in the flowers sticks to their bodies. This pollen gets carried to the next flower they visit.

Not all trees are pollinated in this way. Some trees, like firs and birches, spread their pollen on the wind. They do this by sending billions of pollen grains into the air.

Do all trees have flowers?

Trees that want to attract bees and other insects have big, colorful flowers.

Trees pollinated by the wind often have dangly flowers called catkins, which are easier for the wind to blow.

Trees such as pines and their relatives have cones instead of flowers. Some cones release pollen onto the wind, to drift away and find other cones, which become fertilized and develop seeds.

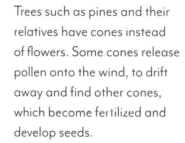

What happens next?

When it's been pollinated, a tree flower can then make fruit with seeds inside. Acorns, berries, nuts, and apples are all examples of this.

The seeds of pines and their relatives grow in cones rather than fruits.

What happens to the fruits and seeds?

Some just fall to the ground, but others can travel long distances. For example, when birds and other animals eat fruits from a tree, the seeds go down into their stomachs. Later, the seeds come out in their poop, often in a different part of the forest.

Cones simply drop their seeds onto the wind.

If any of these seeds find the right kind of soil and shelter, they can grow to become new trees. It's amazing to think that a seed smaller than your little fingernail can turn into a tall, towering tree—but it's true!

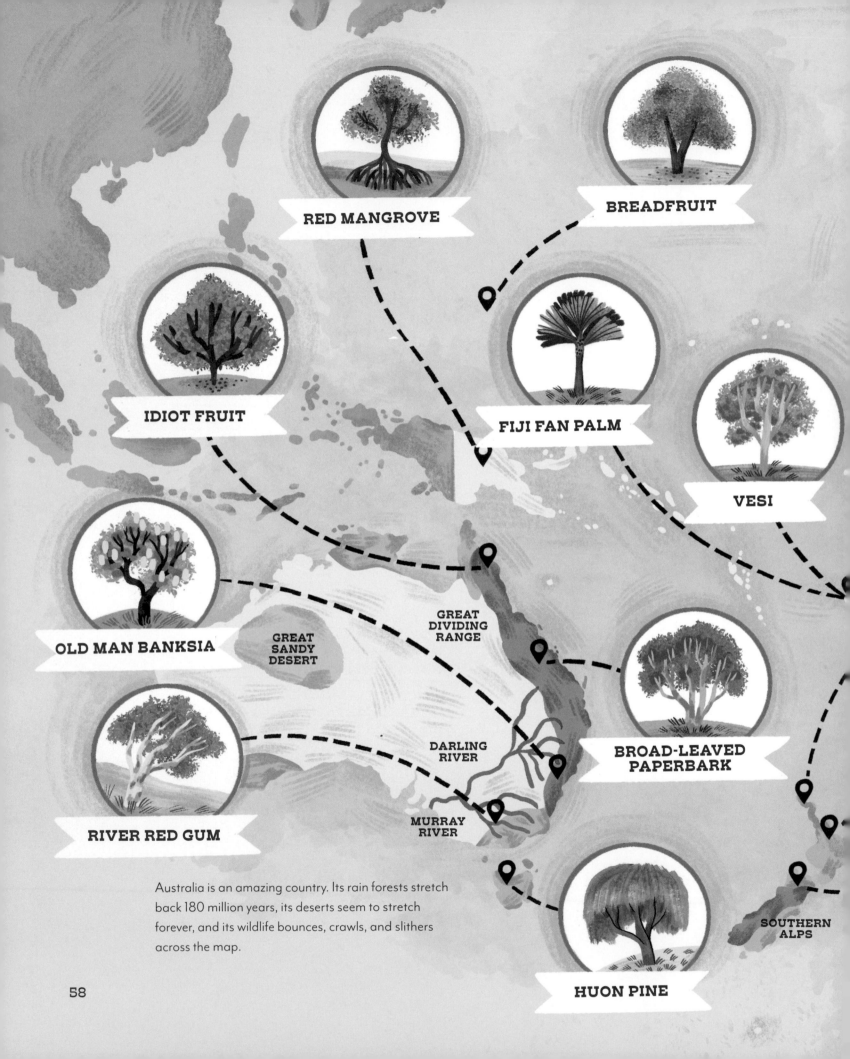

RED MANGROVE

BREADFRUIT

IDIOT FRUIT

FIJI FAN PALM

VESI

OLD MAN BANKSIA

GREAT SANDY DESERT

GREAT DIVIDING RANGE

BROAD-LEAVED PAPERBARK

DARLING RIVER

RIVER RED GUM

MURRAY RIVER

Australia is an amazing country. Its rain forests stretch back 180 million years, its deserts seem to stretch forever, and its wildlife bounces, crawls, and slithers across the map.

SOUTHERN ALPS

HUON PINE

OCEANIA

CANDLENUT

Welcome to Oceania. Picture long beaches, warm sunshine, and blue seas. Australia is by far the biggest country here, but it's just one part of what makes the continent special. New Zealand is filled with sparkling lakes and smoking volcanoes. Papua New Guinea is a world of wild mountains and crashing waves. And the Pacific Ocean is scattered with incredible islands. In every one of these places, there are fascinating trees to be found.

FRANGIPANI

KAURI

TOTARA

SEA TRUMPET

CABBAGE TREE

For thousands of years, many of the countries and islands in this part of the world could only be reached by sea. The first people to live here often arrived by canoe, or in small boats. And what were these canoes and boats made of? Wood! Like in so many places, trees are more than just part of the landscape here. They also play a big part in Oceania's history.

65. River red gum

Think of this Australian tree as a tireless old soldier. The river red gum is a type of eucalyptus tree, with a chunky trunk and flowing branches. It grows next to rivers, creeks, and streams, where its smooth bark gleams in the sunshine. But more than anything, it's a survivor. It can live for more than 1,000 years. It knows how to live in the scorching heat, when the rivers dry up completely, and it knows how to live in stormy floods. It can stand in water for nine months!

Life is easier for the furry fellows in the canopy. These koalas spend almost 20 hours a day asleep, and when they wake up they don't have to look far for food. Eucalyptus leaves are poisonous to humans and most animals, but koalas eat nothing else! The tree's high branches also let these sleepy creatures stay safe from dangers on the ground.

There are almost 900 different types of eucalyptus trees. Almost all of them grow only in Australia. The largest is the mountain ash, which is the tallest flowering tree on the planet.

People have lived here in Australia for tens of thousands of years. They learned long ago that eucalyptus wood is perfect for making canoes, shields, and even boomerangs.

The tree also helps people stay healthy. When its leaves are crushed and soaked, they can be used as a traditional medicine.

Eucalyptus leaves contain a kind of oil, which gives them a nice, minty smell.

61

Australia and New Zealand

Australia and New Zealand sit on either side of the Tasman Sea. Both countries have some very special trees.

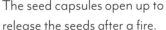

The seed capsules open up to release the seeds after a fire.

66. Old man banksia

Banksia trees are named after Sir Joseph Banks, the first European to collect and study them. There are 173 different banksia species, and this one has tough, wrinkly bark—just like an old man! Wildfires can be a big problem in Australia, so banksias have learned to keep their seeds tightly hidden away, then drop them when the fire stops.

67. Idiot fruit

Australia's Daintree rain forest is ancient and enormous. Here you'll find a world of frogs, ferns, and flowers . . . and a tangle of tropical trees. The idiot fruit tree is one of the oldest. People have found fossils of the tree from 120 million years ago, and today its heavy seeds are still as big as a human fist. The funny name comes from its scientific name, Idiospermum, which means "individuality" and "seed," referring to the tree's peculiar fruit.

68. Broad-leaved paperbark

This flowering tree grows in different parts of Australia, from the busy avenues of Sydney to the tropical swamps of Queensland. Its thin, scruffy bark makes it easy to recognize. Bats and birds drink nectar from its cream flowers, and it's also an important tree for animals like the mahogany glider—a flying possum that needs to jump between tall trunks to move around the forest.

69. Huon pine →

This lovely tree is only found on the Australian island of Tasmania, where it can live for an amazing 3,000 years. Sadly it's now very rare, and there's a risk that climate change might make it extinct. Standing proud on its island at the bottom of the world, the huon pine teaches us that we have to take care of nature.

← 70. Totara

This massive tree towers above the forests of New Zealand. It has stringy bark and sharp, tiny leaves. The people who first lived in New Zealand—the Māori—used the tree's long and straight trunk for their canoes. One totara trunk could make a canoe big enough for 100 people! The wood also has many other uses, because it's light and it doesn't rot.

71. Kauri →

This colossal conifer is a kauri, stretching high into the skies of New Zealand. One very famous kauri is known as Tāne Mahuta, or Lord of the Forest. It's the largest living kauri tree in the country. Tāne Mahuta is so precious that when there was no rain one year, people carried 10,500 gallons of water to the tree to help it stay healthy!

72. Cabbage tree

The long, sword-like leaves of this tree make it simple to spot. It grows in the New Zealand countryside, where its deep, strong roots keep it firmly in the ground. You won't find any cabbages in its branches, but its white berries are eaten by local birds like the kererū, and its leaves are nibbled by wriggly caterpillars.

73. Red mangrove

This strange-looking tree, balancing next to the sea on big flexible roots, is a red mangrove. Most trees find it far too difficult to grow in hot, muddy, salty seawater, but mangroves have a special way of surviving. As the tide goes in and out, they soak up the salt then filter it out through their leaves. This trick is a very successful one. Here in tropical Papua New Guinea, there are mangrove forests bigger than cities!

The seeds of red mangroves are long and thin. They grow on the branches then plop down into the mud like arrows, where they can stay and become new mangrove trees. Some seeds get carried away by the tide to take root on other parts of the coastline. Sadly mangrove forests are among the most threatened and rapidly disappearing natural habitats worldwide.

Above the water, the branches of mangrove forests make a sheltered home for birds like fantails, honeyeaters, and mangrove robins.

Mangroves grow in over 100 countries all across the tropics. Some species have roots that start underground and then poke above the wet mud to find air, like a periscope on a submarine!

Mangrove swamps attract some amazing water wildlife. Mudskippers are fish that can climb onto the shore and shuffle across the mud—they can breathe when they're out of the water! Crabs, shrimp, and other fish like living in underwater mangrove roots too.

Pacific islands

Surrounded by warm blue seas, the islands of the Pacific Ocean are places of long sandy beaches and tropical trees.

74. Vesi

The wood produced by this heavy, slow-growing tree is hard, smooth, and very precious. On the islands of Fiji, people have used it to carve bowls, boats, and even special poles for their temples. But because it takes 80 or 90 years for a vesi tree to grow to its full height, it's very important that we don't cut too many of them down.

75. Sea trumpet

This shady tree is named after its bloom of bright orange flowers, which curl out at the edges like trumpets. The flowers attract butterflies and birds, and the tree's light green leaves are popular with people who catch fish—they can be turned into a dye that makes fishing lines harder for fish to spot.

76. Breadfruit

Here's a fruit you wouldn't want to fall on your head! Breadfruits are big, green, and lumpy, and the trees they grow on have large flapping leaves. They're a popular food on many islands: one tree can grow up to 200 fruits a year, which can be boiled, steamed, or fried for tasty stews, curries, and snacks.

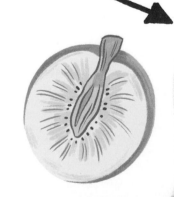

77. Frangipani

On the Pacific Islands—just like in all other parts of the world—some types of trees have always grown here and other types were brought here as seeds or very young trees. One of these is the frangipani, a sweet-smelling tree with shiny leaves and splashy flowers, which was introduced here for its colorful beauty.

78. Fiji fan palm

Like a firework caught in mid bang, the fabulous Fiji fan palm has an explosion of skinny branches with enormous, bright green leaves. Its original home is right here on the Pacific Islands, but people find it so attractive that it's now found in many other hot parts of the world. Its trunk is nice and tall, but it's also flexible enough to sway in the wind.

79. Candlenut

This froth of silvery-green leaves belongs to a candlenut tree. Almost all parts of the tree are useful. The nuts can be cooked and eaten, and the bark, the seeds, the leaves, and even the flowers have been used for traditional medicine on different islands. It's called a candlenut tree because the oily nuts also give off light when they're burned.

80. Lemon

Lemon trees have been planted by people in tropical places all over the world for centuries. The warmth of the Pacific Islands is perfect for them. Their fruits shine like yellow gemstones against the rich dark green of the leaves. You've probably tasted lemon in cakes and candy, but the fruit is also full of healthy vitamin C. Sailors used to drink lemon juice every day to keep them from getting sick on long voyages.

67

The importance of trees

Trees have been growing on our planet for much, much longer than humans have lived here. Like the mountains and oceans, they're part of an ancient, wilder world. This is just one of the reasons why trees are something for us to treasure.

For many thousands of years, people have gathered at trees to meet, to talk, to celebrate, and even to give thanks to their gods. In some places, trees are just as important as temples, churches, and other religious buildings. Stories and tales grow around these trees, and they help people feel a close connection to nature.

Trees help us in many other ways. On a hot day, they give humans and animals somewhere to escape from the heat of the sun. On a rainy day, they give us somewhere to shelter from the bad weather. They also give us natural climbing frames to play on!

Most important of all, they make our air cleaner, help wildlife, and turn Earth into a greener, more beautiful place.

What trees give us

Trees aren't just important to us for natural, cultural, and spiritual reasons. They also provide us with wood that we can make into a wide variety of objects, from foods and medicines to furniture and books! Take a look at some of the many things that trees give us.

Wood

We use wood in our buildings, our furniture, our toys, our musical instruments, our pencils, and hundreds of other things.

Food

A lot of the food that we eat comes from trees: fantastic fruits, crunchy nuts, and other yummy things like chocolate and maple syrup.

Medicine & materials

In many parts of the world, trees give us natural medicine that can help us when we're not well. They also give us materials such as rubber, cork, and cardboard. They even give us paper—the book that you're reading wouldn't exist without trees!

Why trees need our help

Trees do so much for the planet. They give homes to plants and animals, make life easier for us as humans, and help reduce the effects of climate change. So when we chop down too many trees, it can be a very big problem.

Deforestation and pollution

In some parts of the world, huge numbers of trees are being cut down so that the land underneath can be used for other things, like giant farms and factories. Even enormous jungles like the Amazon are getting smaller every month. This means birds and animals are losing their habitats and the planet is losing its precious green areas. Another problem is that when our air, soil, and rivers become polluted, this harms trees too.
It's important that we do what we can to help.

Managed forests

We can use wood responsibly, making it a very eco-friendly material, by growing trees in specially managed forests. When these are chopped down, other trees are planted to replace them. The trees that were used to make the paper for this book were grown this way.

So what can we do?

There are different things we can do to help trees have a healthy future.

Be careful

Try not to waste paper or cardboard. If it can be used again, keep it for later instead of putting it in the trash. If you do have to throw it away, make sure it will be recycled.

Try growing seeds in old toilet rolls.

Be green

Living a green life and keeping nature clean helps trees. And if you can encourage your friends and family to do the same, that's even better!

Try traveling by bike instead of by car.

Join a campaign

Organizations like the Rainforest Trust, Greenpeace, and Friends of the Earth work hard to stop too many trees and forests from being cut down. By supporting them, you'll be helping too.

Plant trees

One of the very best things you can do is to plant trees yourself. In many cities, towns, and villages around the world, there are local tree-planting projects you can join. If there isn't one close to you, maybe you could start a project of your own? Watching a tree grow bigger—slowly but surely, year by year—is a wonderful thing.

Index